Do You Have a Secret?

Pamela Russell
&
Beth Stone

ILLUSTRATIONS BY MARY MCKEE

CompCare® publications

Do You Have a Secret?

©1986 Bonita Productions, Inc.

All rights reserved.
Published in the United States
by CompCare Publications,
a division of Comprehensive Care Corporation

Reproduction in whole or part, in any form, including storage
in memory device systems, is forbidden without written permission
... except that portions may be used in broadcast or printed
commentary or review when attributed fully to author and
publication by names.

Library of Congress Cataloging-in-Publication Data

Stone, Beth, 1944-
Do you have a secret?

Summary: Discusses, in simple text and illustrations,
good and bad secrets, how to differentiate between
them, and how not to keep bad secrets to oneself.
1. Child abuse—Juvenile literature. 2. Child
abuse—Prevention—Juvenile literature. [1. Child
abuse. 2. Secrets] I. Russell, Pamela, 1947-
II. McKee, Mary (Mary Michele), ill. III. Title.
HV713.S78 1986   362.7'044   85-27986
ISBN 0-89638-098-X

Cover and interior design by Mary McKee

Inquiries, orders, and catalog requests should be addressed to
CompCare Publications
2415 Annapolis Lane
Minneapolis, Minnesota 55441
Call toll-free 800/328-3330
(Minnesota residents 612/559-4800)

Adult Guide

This book helps adults talk with children about the difficult subject of sexual abuse. For a child who has been abused by a non-family member, the book opens the door for the child to tell his parents and seek help. For a child who has been abused by a family member, it suggests important resources. Without scaring a child who is not a victim, the book gives valuable information every child needs in order to talk about things that are troubling.

The pledge to secrecy is the one thing all sexually abused children have in common. Since the sexual abuser is usually a relative or person known to the child, the abuse is often a slow process which begins during the child's pre-school or early childhood years. For the abuse to continue, the secret must be maintained. The emotional stress of keeping the secret can be more damaging than the actual abuse. The terrible secret contributes to the devastating psychological damage to the child.

The secret must be told if the child is to find a way out of the pattern of abuse. **Do You Have a Secret?** helps the child understand this. It points out individuals to whom the child can safely tell the secret if the abuse is perpetrated by someone in the home and no family member is willing or able to stop it.

This book also helps a young child know he or she is not the only one who has experienced abuse. Abuse can happen in any kind of home, at any socio-economic level.

People in the field of human services—teachers, coaches, counselors, health professionals, and others—are legally required to report incidents of abuse to a local child welfare agency. These agencies will do everything possible to protect the child, restore the abuser to healthy, positive behavior, and keep the family together when the abuser is a family member.

Adult Guide

Adults must be alert to signs and symptoms of sexual abuse, such as:

- frequent absences from school
- a sudden drop in grades
- social isolation
- depression
- eating disorders—obesity, anorexia
- bedwetting
- pelvic inflammation
- phobias
- compulsive need to be clean
- making self unattractive
- sleep disturbances
- sleeping in school
- running away
- sexual misbehavior

These signs may also indicate areas of concern that are not related to sexual abuse.

Adult Guide

This book contains information that is important for any child. But if you observe signs like these or have any other reason to suspect abuse, read this book with the child. If the child confides in you, you must:

- believe the child
- be warm and supportive
- talk in private and in his or her own vocabulary
- affirm the "rightness" of telling the secret
- emphasize that the child is not responsible for the act or situation
- avoid focusing on the abuser
- never condemn the abuser to the child
- report the situation immediately to a child welfare agency

With awareness and action, we **can** stop this critical problem of child abuse. We must be willing to believe that abuse does happen—with alarming frequency.

Beth Stone and Pamela Russell

Do you have a secret?

How do you feel when you hear your secret inside your head? Does your secret put a smile on your face and make you feel happy?

Maybe your secret
is that your grandmother
is coming for a visit.

Your secret might be a picture you are drawing for your mother.

Or your secret might be a gift you bought for your sister's birthday.

Your secret may be
that you have a friend
no one else can see.

These are secrets that make you happy when you think about them.

But some secrets make boys and girls feel unhappy. Do you have a secret that makes you feel sad or hurt or afraid? Do you have a secret you are scared to tell because you think it may be bad?

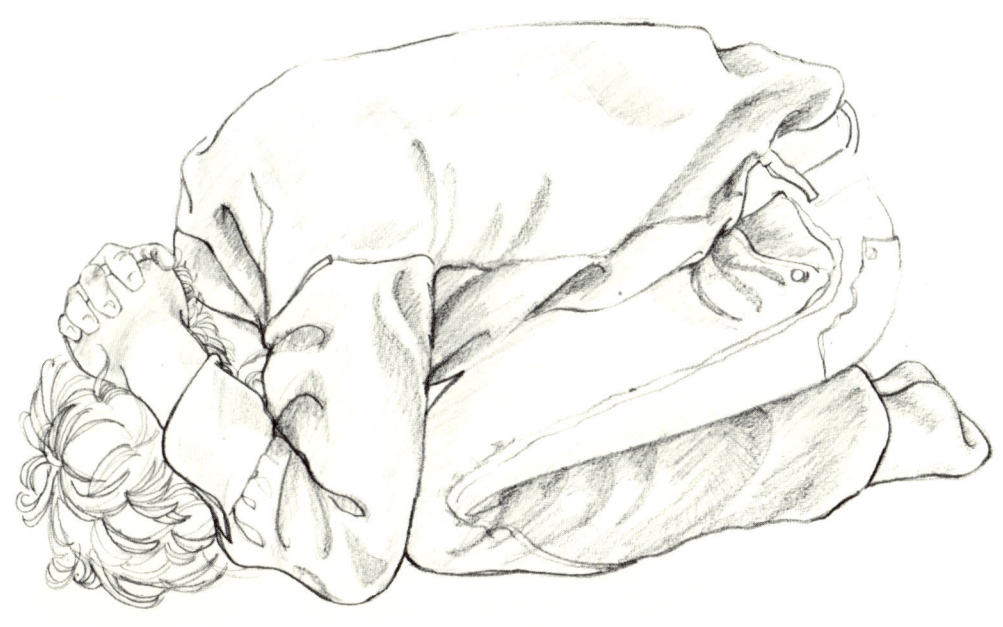

Does your secret
make you want to
hide and cry?

Maybe a big person did something that was wrong. Maybe a stranger made you afraid—or perhaps it was someone you know and feel you must obey. That person may have said to you, "Don't tell anyone."

But you **MUST**
tell a grown-up
you trust and ask that person to help you. If the person who makes you keep the unhappy secret is a stranger or someone who doesn't live with you, tell your mother or your father. Then the scary secret will not make you feel so afraid.

Your scary secret might be that someone you love, perhaps even someone in your family, touches you in a way that hurts or that makes you unhappy and afraid. Your body belongs to YOU. It is okay to say, "NO!" if you do not want someone to touch you. Maybe you cannot stop that person from touching you because you are smaller. Maybe the person says, "This is our secret. Don't tell!" The secret makes you feel bad.

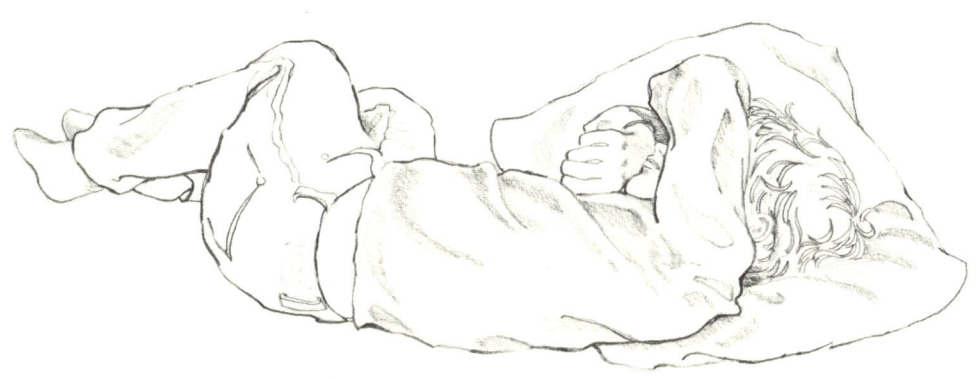

YOU are not bad because you have a scary secret.
YOU are not bad if someone hurt you.
YOU are not bad if someone touched you and made you afraid.

    THAT PERSON is wrong and must stop.

Scary secrets tie you up inside. They won't let you grow. Scary secrets can keep you awake at night. They can make you feel very lonely or unhappy. Thinking about scary secrets can give you poor grades in school. Unhappy secrets can even make you sick!

Does your secret make you hurt inside?
Maybe you want to tell someone your secret,
but you are afraid you will get into trouble.
Are you afraid someone will think you
have been bad? Are you afraid
someone will hurt you or
someone you love if you tell?

You are not the only one who has an unhappy secret. Many other children do, too. Some people you know have helped other children who had scary secrets like yours. These people can help you, too. You must tell someone you trust what has happened to you.

Telling the scary secret to a special friend will make you feel happier. You have many special friends who care about you and will help you. The person who gave you this book is your special friend who cares about you. Tell that person you have a scary secret.

Your doctor is a special friend
who cares about you.
When you have a problem you can
ask your special friend to help.

The school nurse and your teacher, principal, and counselor care about you. Your minister and Sunday school teacher care about you, too. You can tell your secret to them.

If one person you tell
does not believe you
or help you, tell someone else.

There is a special friend you can talk to on the telephone by dialing:

1-800-422-4453.

This person has helped many boys and girls who had secrets like yours. The person on the telephone will help you.

You MUST tell
the scary secret,
even if a big person told you
never to tell anyone. Even if that person
has told you that you—or someone you love—
will be hurt if you tell.

After you tell your unhappy secret
you will have a happy new secret.
You will know you have a
special friend who cares
about making you feel happy.

Secrets are good to keep if they make you feel happy. Scary secrets are not good to keep.

About the Authors

Pamela Russell is a Certified Social Worker (Advanced Clinical Practitioner) and Licensed Counselor in private practice in Paris, Texas. She is executive director of Life Anew, Inc., adoption agency, and also a consultant for McCuistion Regional Medical Center, Paris, Texas, and Goodland Presbyterian Childrens' Home in Hugo, Oklahoma.

Her academic degrees include a B.S. from Oklahoma State University and a M.S.S.W. from the University of Texas at Arlington. She is a candidate for a doctoral degree in Marriage and Family Therapy at East Texas State University. For several years she has been associated with the Texas Department of Human Resources—as a child protective services worker, social services supervisor, and program director. Currently she is under contract with the department, counseling sexually abused victims and perpetrators. She has served on the Social Work Advisory Board of East Texas State University; Alcohol and Drug Abuse Council, Paris, Texas; Methodist Day Care Center, Clarksville, Texas; East Texas Police Academy, Kilgore College. She is the author of professional articles and has been a speaker—often on the subject of child abuse—for organizations on local, state, and national levels.

She and her husband, Mike, are parents of two children.

Beth Stone is the pen name of Bonnie Beth Burgess Neely, free-lance journalist and author of the newspaper feature on parent-child relationships, "Formulas for Fun," which has appeared regularly in twenty-five newspapers since 1979. Formerly women's feature writer for *The Greenville (South Carolina) News-Piedmont* and editor of a weekly newspaper, she is the author of *ParenTips*, a 1986 title from Simon and Schuster's Pocket Books.

She was a project coordinator and research writer for *"Children of Portugal,"* a series of nine documentaries filmed in Portugal for Hawaiian Educational Television, and executive producer and script writer for a film documentary, *Ageless Arts of Portugal*. Currently she is working toward a master's degree in photography and journalism at East Texas State University.

Besides managing her professional pursuits, she's a Scout leader, a pianist, a teacher of needle arts and crafts, and a former board member of WillowCreek Children's Home.

She attended Queens College in Charlotte, North Carolina, and Furman University, and graduated from Southern Methodist University with a B.A. in English and education.

She and her husband, Bill, have three children.